The History and Activities of the

REVOLUTIONARY WAR

Margaret C. Hall

Heinemann Library
Chicago, Illinois

Customer Service 888-454-2279
Visit our website at www.heinemannraintree.com

Designed by Richard Parker and Tinstar Design Ltd (www.tinstar.co.uk)
Printed and bound in China by CTPS

12 11 10
10 9 8 7 6 5 4 3

ISBN 13: 9781403460585 (PB)

Library of Congress Cataloging-in-Publication Data

Hall, Margaret, 1947-
  The history and activities of the Revolutionary War / Margaret C. Hall.
     p. cm. -- (Hands-on American history)
  Includes bibliographical references and index.
  ISBN 1-4034-6051-5 -- ISBN 1-4034-6058-2 (pbk.)
  1. United States--History--Colonial period, ca. 1600-1775--Study and
teaching--Activity programs--Juvenile literature. 2. United
States--History--Revolution, 1775-1783--Study and teaching--Activity
programs--Juvenile literature. I. Title. II. Series.
  E188.H24 2006
  973.2--dc22
                                    2004003880

Acknowledgments
The author and publishers are grateful to the following for permission to reproduce copyright material:
Bridgeman Art Library pp. 16 (Massachusetts Historical Society, Boston, MA, USA), 9 (Hall of
Representatives, Washington D.C., USA); Corbis pp. 10, 14, 15, 20 (Bettmann); Getty Images p. 6
(MPI/Stringer); Harcourt Education pp. 17, 19, 23, 24, 29 (Janet Moran); Mary Evans Picture Library
pp. 7 (Douglas McCarthy), 11 (Fae Fallon (colorist)), 5, 13; North Wind Picture Archives p. 26; Peter
Newark's American Pictures p. 12.

Cover photographs by Bridgeman Art Library/New York Historical Society and Art Archive

Every effort has been made to contact copyright holders of any material reproduced in this book.
Any omissions will be rectified in subsequent printings if notice is given to the publishers.

Contents

Some words are shown in bold, **like this**. You can find out
what they mean by looking in the glossary.

Chapter 1: Revolution and Independence

In the early 1600s, England created **colonies** in North America. The English wanted to increase their wealth and power by using the resources of this new territory. The people of Spain and France wanted to do the same thing. These two countries competed with England for control of North America.

From 1754 to 1763, English and colonial soldiers fought against French and Native American troops in the French and Indian War. When France surrendered, England gained control of most of the land east of the Mississippi River. After the war, many North American colonists wanted more independence. At the same time, England passed a series of laws trying to strengthen its power over the colonies.

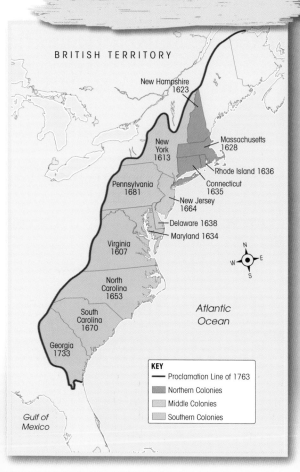

This map shows the thirteen original American colonies.

BRITISH TERRITORY

New Hampshire 1623

New York 1613

Massachusetts 1628

Rhode Island 1636

Connecticut 1635

Pennsylvania 1681

New Jersey 1664

Delaware 1638

Maryland 1634

Virginia 1607

North Carolina 1653

South Carolina 1670

Georgia 1733

Atlantic Ocean

Gulf of Mexico

KEY
— Proclamation Line of 1763
■ Northern Colonies
■ Middle Colonies
■ Southern Colonies

TIME LINE

1754	1763	1765	1767	1773
French and Indian War begins.	French and Indian War ends.	British tax American paper goods.	British Acts tax tea and other goods.	Colonists throw British tea into Boston harbor; British close Boston harbor.

Protesting taxes

In 1765 England's government passed the Stamp Act. This law required colonists to buy a special stamp for every piece of printed paper they used. The government also passed the Townshend Acts, which made colonists pay taxes when they bought lead, glass, paper, paint, or tea from England.

These and other laws upset colonists because they did not have the right to vote for the government that was charging them taxes. In 1773 some colonists in Boston protested the tea tax by dressing like Native Americans and dumping a huge load of tea off of a British ship into the harbor. This protest became known as the Boston Tea Party.

England's King George III ordered the port of Boston closed. No ships could enter or leave the harbor. This put a lot of colonists out of work. They couldn't fish, unload cargo, or send goods to other places.

This is an example of the stamp forced on the colonies.

1774	1775	1776	1781	1787
First Continental Congress meets.	Revolutionary War begins.	Declaration of Independence written.	French troops help Continental Army defeat England.	United States of America adopts a **constitution.**

The **colonists'** struggle for independence eventually led to war. On April 19, 1775, British and American soldiers fought battles in the towns of Lexington and Concord, Massachusetts. It was the beginning of the American Revolution, or Revolutionary War.

In May 1775, General George Washington commanded the Continental Army against British troops at Bunker Hill in Massachusetts. After a day of battle, the Americans ran out of **ammunition** for their weapons and had to retreat. That left the British in control of Boston.

After the Battle of Bunker Hill, the Continental Congress voted to break free of England. Thomas Jefferson wrote a document explaining that the Americans believed the colonies were "free and independent states." On July 4, 1776, the representatives signed this Declaration of Independence.

While General Washington sent troops north into Canada, the British navy attacked cities up and down the Atlantic coast. Fighting continued for years. Battles raged in Massachusetts, New York, New Jersey, Virginia, North Carolina, and the Ohio Territory.

A battle scene from the French and Indian War.

The Americans seemed to have little chance of winning the war. The Continental Army was made up of farmers and shopkeepers, not trained soldiers. They had little money for uniforms, weapons, or ammunition. British soldiers, on the other hand, were well trained. They also had plenty of food and ammunition.

King George III

In 1777 the Americans won an important battle at Saratoga, New York. This made King Louis XVI of France take an interest in the war. France and England were still enemies, so Louis decided to send money and soldiers to help the Americans.

Even with the help of the French, the fighting continued. In 1781 the British army marched toward Yorktown, Virginia. British leaders were sure they could win a battle there and end the war. General Washington got word that more French troops were sailing toward Yorktown to help the Americans. He sent his troops south to Yorktown. When the French ships arrived, they blocked the Yorktown harbor. The British Army was trapped. After days of battle, they surrendered. America had won its independence.

After the Revolution

Even after the British surrendered, it took more than a year for the war to officially end. On September 3, 1783, American and British leaders signed a peace **treaty**. The treaty outlined the boundaries of the United States of America. The new nation stretched from the Atlantic Ocean west to the Mississippi River. It went from the Great Lakes south to close to Florida.

Becoming independent meant more than winning the war. The thirteen **colonies** had always been separate. Their leaders were not used to acting together, like one nation. Members of the Continental Congress knew they needed a plan for how the country should be governed, or ruled.

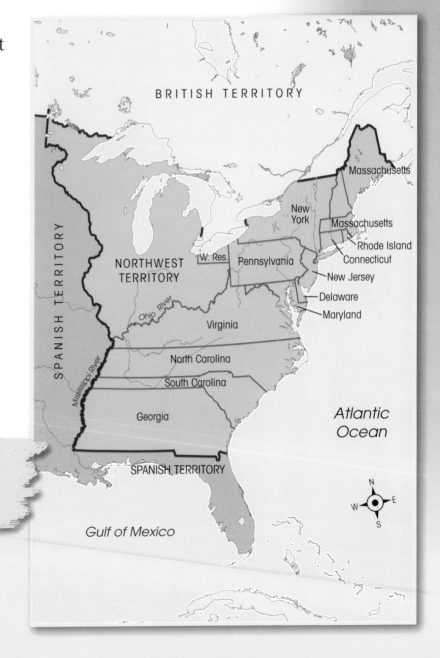

This map shows the boundaries of the U.S. in 1783.

BRITISH TERRITORY

SPANISH TERRITORY

NORTHWEST TERRITORY

W. Res.

Pennsylvania

New York

Massachusetts

Massachusetts

Rhode Island

Connecticut

New Jersey

Delaware

Maryland

Ohio River

Virginia

North Carolina

South Carolina

Georgia

Mississippi River

SPANISH TERRITORY

Atlantic Ocean

Gulf of Mexico

N E W S

George Washington presiding at the signing of the Constitution of the United States in Philadelphia on Sept. 17th 1787.

In 1787 a Constitutional Convention met in Philadelphia. The members of this group met for months. They talked about what kind of leader the nation should have. They talked about how laws would be made and enforced. The representatives wrote a **constitution**, or plan for a new kind of government. The constitution said that the United States of America was a **democracy**. That meant the people would vote to choose their leaders.

Before the constitution could become official, people in at least nine of the thirteen states had to vote for it. By June 1788, the constitution was approved. In 1789 George Washington was elected the first president of the United States of America.

Chapter 2: Life During Wartime

Life of a Continental soldier

Many of the soldiers in George Washington's Continental Army came from the poorer ranks of society. Some were forced into the army. Others joined the army because they had few other opportunities. Some were **indentured servants** who were sent to war in place of their masters. Wealthy men could pay others to fight for them. Most of the Continental soldiers were young. In some communities, many boys as young as fifteen or sixteen served in the Continental Army.

One such soldier was Private Joseph Plumb Martin. Martin was born on November 21, 1760. He joined the Massachusetts state militia when he was fifteen and served in the Continental Army from 1777 to 1783. Martin was even there when the British surrendered at Yorktown in 1781.

The Battle of Bunker Hill

This painting shows the British surrendering at Yorktown. George Washington is in the blue coat, holding his hat.

In 1830, when he was 70, Martin wrote a book about his experiences called *Private Yankee Doodle: Being a Narrative of Some of the Adventures, Dangers, and Sufferings of a Revolutionary Soldier.* The book tells of the problems the soldiers faced, including harsh winters, long marches, fierce battles, hunger, lack of clothes and equipment, and having no money to buy the things they needed.

"I procured [got] a small piece of raw cowhide and made myself a pair of moccasins, which kept my feet (while they lasted) from the frozen ground, although, as I well remember, the hard edges so galled [rubbed] my ankles, while on a march, that it was with much difficulty and pain that I could wear them afterwards. The only alternative I had was to endure this inconvenience or to go barefoot, as hundreds of my companions had to, till they might be tracked by their blood upon the rough frozen ground. But hunger, nakedness and sore shins were not the only difficulties we had at that time to encounter. We had hard duty to perform and little or no strength to perform it with."
– Joseph Plumb Martin, Continental Army

The struggle at home

The war years were also difficult for the **colonists** who weren't soldiers. When men and boys joined the army, women, children, and the elderly were left behind to keep farms and businesses running.

Most colonists were farmers. They raised food for themselves and for people who lived in cities such as Boston, Philadelphia, and New York. As soldiers marched through the colonies, they purchased or took the food they needed from nearby farms and shops. Sometimes that meant there wasn't enough food for everyone in the area.

War meant doing without other supplies as well. Sometimes this was by choice. For example, some patriots refused to buy English cloth. Instead, women spun thread and wove their own cloth.

No one could completely avoid the war. Battles were fought on farms and in cities and towns. Homes were sometimes turned into temporary hospitals for the wounded. Neighbors, friends, and even families were divided by the war.

Farmland in Virginia in the 1700s.

Molly Pitcher takes her wounded husband's place as artillery person.

Not all colonists wanted independence from England. About one out of every three colonists was loyal to the English king. In some cases, members of the same family fought on opposite sides of the war.

Thousands of people were killed or died of disease during the war. Many more suffered and sacrificed in ways that have not been recorded by history. But despite its human cost, many people all over the world saw the Revolutionary War as a victory for the ideals of freedom and liberty.

FAMILIES AT WAR

Some women traveled with their husbands in the Continental Army. Many had children with them, too. The women cooked, sewed, and did laundry for the troops. Others cared for wounded soldiers. Children carried water, collected firewood, and passed along messages. Some women even joined in the fighting. After her husband was killed, Margaret Corbin took his weapon and kept shooting at the British.

Chapter 3: Games and Other Entertainment

Adult men got together in taverns or coffeehouses to discuss politics and the war. They played cards and listened to music. Women visited each other at home or in church. They often worked on sewing projects while talking. Reading was popular, but books were expensive. In the 1700s a book cost about $66 in today's money. To save money, people borrowed books from libraries.

Children

Children who lived during **colonial** times did not have as much time for play as children do today. Most of them had chores to do on the family farm every day before and after school. But in the play time that they did have, they enjoyed a variety of games and toys. Some of the colonial games and toys are still popular today, while others have been almost forgotten.

There were no toy factories or stores in the American colonies. Most of the toys that children played with were homemade. Dolls were made from many different things, including cornhusks, pinecones, and old rags. Dried apples were sometimes used to make faces for the dolls.

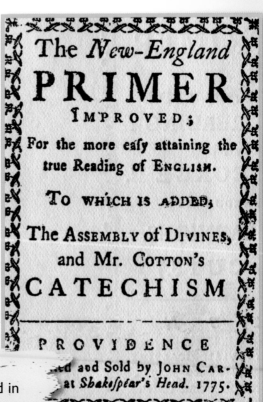

The *New-England* PRIMER IMPROVED; For the more easy attaining the true Reading of ENGLISH.

To WHICH IS ADDED,

The ASSEMBLY of DIVINES, and Mr. COTTON's CATECHISM

PROVIDENCE

...d and Sold by JOHN CAR- ...at Shakespear's Head. 1775.

This textbook was used in Colonial schools.

Another popular toy was the rolling hoop. Children used a hoop from an old barrel and ran along beside it with a stick to keep it rolling. They saw how far it would roll, or sometimes they had races with their hoops. Colonial children also played with marbles, kites, balls, jump ropes, and spinning tops.

Kids often played games more than they played with toys. Children who lived during the Revolutionary War played many games that kids still play today. They ran races and played hopscotch, leapfrog, checkers, and hide-and-seek. They played a game called nine pins, which was similar to bowling. They sat the pins down on the lawn and try to knock them over with a wooden ball. They also played a game called quoits, which was similar to horseshoes.

Hoops were a popular Colonial toy.

Chapter 4: Hands-on History

The activities and recipes in this section of the book will help give you an idea of what life was like for people during the Revolutionary War.

Recipe: Make a Teatime Treat

In **colonial** times, tea was expensive, so colonists stored it in locked boxes called tea caddies. To make tea, colonists grated a few leaves and poured boiling water over them. When the British began charging a tax on tea, many colonists stopped drinking it rather than pay the tax. They made tea substitutes by drying berries and leaves of plants like sage. They also made biscuits to have with their tea. These were served with butter, or for a special occasion, possibly apple butter or fruit spread.

Baking powder did not exist in colonial times, so colonial biscuits would have been flatter than modern biscuits.

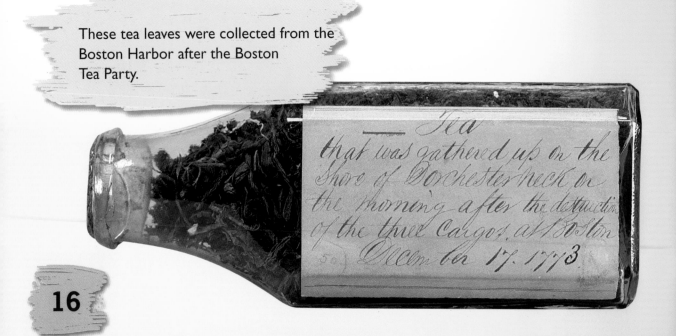

These tea leaves were collected from the Boston Harbor after the Boston Tea Party.

INGREDIENTS AND SUPPLIES

- mixing bowl and spoons
- measuring cups
- greased cookie sheet
- wax paper
- rolling pin
- 2 cups (435 grams) flour
- 4 teaspoons (20 milliliters)
- baking powder
- 1/2 teaspoon (2 1/2 milliliters) salt
- 1/4 cup (59 milliliters) softened butter
- 1/4 cup (59 milliliters) milk

1. Preheat the oven to 450°.

2. Combine the flour, baking powder, and salt in a mixing bowl.

3. Add the butter and mix until crumbly.

4. Add the milk and stir.

5. Sprinkle flour on the wax paper to prevent sticking. Roll the mixture out on the wax paper. The dough should be about 1 inch thick.

6. Use the open end of a small juice glass to cut round biscuit shapes.

7. Place the biscuits on the cookie sheet and bake for 10 to 15 minutes.

   Serve the biscuits with blackberry or raspberry tea to recreate a colonial "tea substitute."

Activity: Take a Survey

When he was young, George Washington worked as a surveyor. He measured land claimed by England in North America and made maps based on the measurements. You can conduct a survey of your own. Measure and map an area near your home or school.

George Washington surveying land.

SUPPLIES

- 12-foot (3.65-meter) tape measure
- 6-8 small marking cones or garden stakes
- paper and pencil (consider using graph paper)
- poster paper
- markers

WARNING!

Make sure to read all instructions before beginning the project.

1. Choose an area to survey. It can be the school playground, your backyard, or any other outdoor area.

2. On paper, make a sketch of the area that you will be surveying. (See picture A)

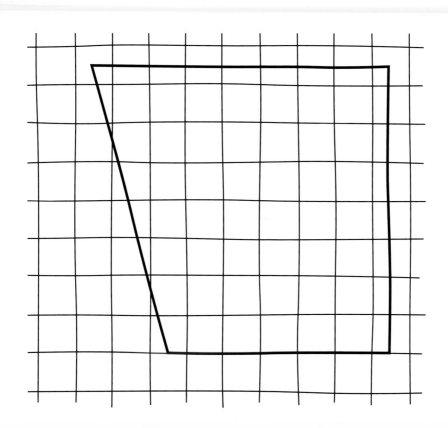

A

3. Place a cone (or stake) in one corner of the area to mark your starting point. Draw the cone on your sketch in the correct place.

4. Place a cone at the next nearest corner of the area. Working with a partner, measure from the first cone along the side of the area to your new cone. Record the measurement along that part of your sketch. (See picture B)

5. Place a third cone at the next corner. Measure the distance between the two cones. Record your measurement and add to your sketch. Continue until all the sides have been measured.

6. Measure and sketch features such as fences, sidewalks, and other details. Then collect the cones. (See picture C)

7. Use your measurements and sketch to make a map of the area on poster paper. Check and make sure that you drew the short sides correctly compared to the long sides.

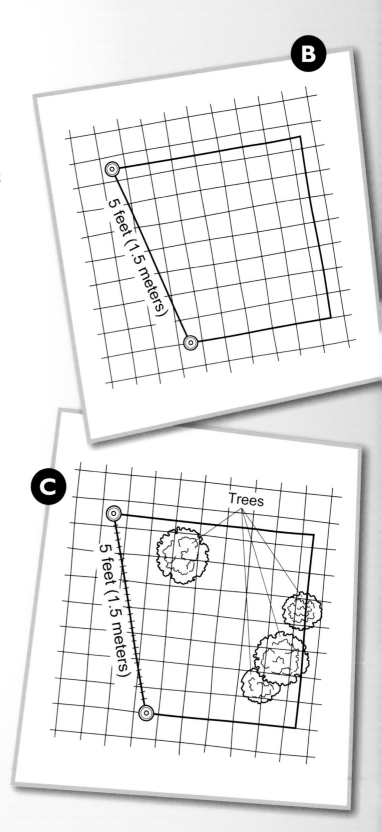

8. Label the map and add symbols
   to show where trees, buildings,
   and other objects are located.
   Add a key that explains what
   each symbol means. *Why would
   the people in a new country
   need to survey the land?*

Activity: Play Quoits

The game of quoits was similar to the game of horseshoes. Kids would try to toss leather, rope, or iron rings over a stake in the ground. They scored points based on how close their rings landed to the stake.

SUPPLIES

- 36-inch (90-centimeter) square of cardboard
- red and black markers
- clay
- unsharpened pencil
- four plastic coffee-can lids or plastic rings
- craft knife

1. **Make the game board.** With markers, copy the design in picture A on a piece of cardboard.

2. **Make a ball of clay and stick it to the cardboard at the center.** Anchor the pencil in the clay as shown. (See picture B)

3. **Ask an adult to cut the middle out of the coffee can lids to make rings.**

4. **Take turns trying to throw the rings over the pencil.** Keep score as shown on the chart. The players with the highest score wins. *Is it more fun to buy a game or make your own?*

If the ring lands...	You score...
Over the pencil	30 points
Partly in the center, partly in the red ring	20 points
Completely in the red ring	15 points
Partly in the red ring, partly in the black border	10 points
Partly in the black border	5 points

A

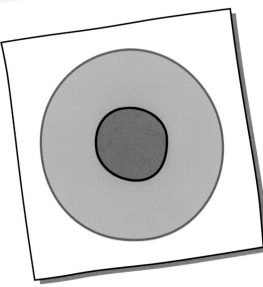

B

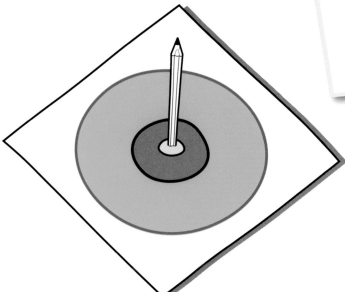

Craft: Create a Silhouette

In the 1700s, there were no cameras. Some people hired artists to paint their portraits, but that was expensive. A less expensive way to get an image of a person was to hire someone to cut a silhouette, or outline, shaped like the side-view of a person's face. A good silhouette maker could cut out a silhouette without drawing a single line. He just cut the paper as he looked at the person. Using light and shadows makes it easier to cut a silhouette. You can make one of a friend or family member. Then have that person make a silhouette of you.

Dolley and James Madison silhouettes, done from life.

SUPPLIES

- 2 pieces of white construction paper
- 2 pieces of black construction paper
- tape
- bright lamp or overhead projector
- pencil or crayon
- scissors
- glue

To make a white silhouette:

1. Place a chair about 18 inches (46 centimeters) from a blank wall. Ask your partner to sit sideways in the chair. Then tape the white paper to the wall at the same height as the person's head.

2. Place the light behind the chair. Move it backward or forward until the shadow of the person's head fits on the paper taped to the wall. (See picture A)

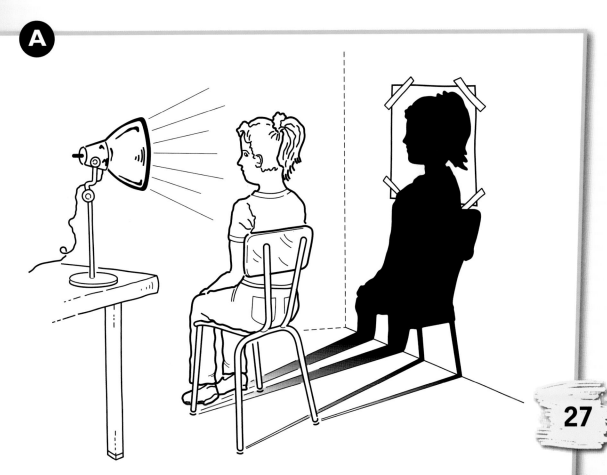

A

3. Stand to one side so you don't block the light. With a pencil, trace the outline of the shadow.

4. Cut out the shape and glue it to the center of the black paper. (See picture B)

To make a black silhouette, use the same process, but this time, tape black paper to the wall. It might be difficult to draw on the black paper and see the line. *What are some ways you can solve this problem?*

B

Glossary

ammunition bullets or other objects that are fired from a weapon

colony land owned or ruled by another country. A *colonist* is someone who lives in a colony.

constitution written plan for a new government

democracy government ruled by its citizens

indentured servant servant who works until a debt is paid off. Indentured servants were often forced into being servants.

treaty agreement between two countries, usually ending or preventing a war

More Books to Read

Anderson, Dale. *The American Revolution*. Chicago: Raintree, 2002.

Smolinski, Diane. *Americans at War: Revolutionary War*. Chicago: Heinemann, 2001.

A Note to Teachers

The instructions for these projects are designed to allow students to work as independently as possible. However, it is always a good idea to make a prototype before assigning any project, so that students can see how their own work will look when completed. Prior to introducing these projects, teachers should collect and prepare the materials and be ready for any modifications that may be necessary. Participating in the project-making process will help teachers understand the directions and be ready to assist students with difficult steps. Teachers might also choose to adapt or modify the lessons to better suit the needs of an individual student or class. No one knows what levels of achievement students will reach better than their teacher.

While it is preferable for students to work as independently as possible, there is some flexibility in regards to project materials and tools. They can vary according to what is available. For instance, while standard white glue may be most familiar to students, there might be times when a teacher will choose to speed up a project by using a hot glue gun to fasten materials for students. Likewise, while a project may call for leather cord, it is feasible in most instances to substitute vinyl cord or even yarn or rope. Acrylic paint may be recommended because it adheres better to a material like felt or plastic, but other types of paint would be useable as well. Circles can be drawn with a compass, or simply by tracing a cup, roll of tape, or other circular object. Obviously, allowing students a broad spectrum of creativity and opportunities to problem-solve within the parameters of a given project will encourage their critical thinking skills most fully.

Each project contains an italicized question somewhere in the directions. These questions are meant to be thought-provoking and promote discussion while students work on the project.

Index